Building Madness

By Kate Danley

Winner of the 2016 Panowski Playwriting Award

CAST OF CHARACTERS

<u>Trixie Fuller</u>: the dizzy secretary of TF Architecture

<u>Paul Fielding</u>: a down-to-earth, easy-going architect with a casual charisma

<u>Max Marshall</u>: a passionate and ridiculously insecure architect

<u>Gwen Gladwell</u>: a witty, smart socialite who is a fool when it comes to love

<u>Ruby Deleoni</u>: the va-va-va-voom head of the Deleoni family

<u>Vito Deleoni</u>: Ruby's nephew. A tough but dim mobster.

TIME

The 1930s.

SETTING

For the purposes of the reader, imagine the office of TF Architects with an art deco flair. Stage right is the door to the building hallway. Center stage is the desk of Trixie Fuller. Behind her up stage right is the door to Paul Fielding's office, up stage left is Max Marshall. Stage left is a door to the office kitchen. There is a low balustrade behind Trixie's desk separating the reception area from the offices. In the space between the balustrade and the back wall is work area with a drafting table, a table with building models, blueprints hanging from the walls, and some filing cabinets. Unfiled paperwork is lying on every surface. Center stage on the back wall is a massive window which shows off the skyscrapers of the city. For the restaurant scenes, a table and suggestive set dressing (a potted plant or a single statue) are brought out and set either downstage right or left.

SYNOPSIS OF SCENES

ACT I - Scene 1
Office of TF Architecture, Monday morning

ACT I - Scene 2
Office of TF Architecture,
late-morning, several days later

ACT I - Scene 3
Cafe, noon, same day

ACT I - Scene 4
Office of TF Architecture, morning, next day

ACT I - Scene 5
Office of TF Architecture, mid-morning the next week

ACT II - Scene 1
The Grove Super Club, evening, same day

ACT II - Scene 2
Office of TF Architecture, morning, next day

ACT II - Scene 3
Office of TF Architecture,
mid-morning, several days later

ACT II - Scene 4
Office of TF Architecture, next day

ACT I

Scene 1

A Monday morning. Lights come up on the offices of TF Architects. The room is a mess, covered in unfiled paperwork. Secretary TRIXIE FULLER sits at her desk happily typing badly. As she slowly picks out the keysy, PAUL FIELDING enters the room. He throws his hat and it lands on the hat rack.

PAUL: Morning, Trixie!

TRIXIE: And a happy Monday morning to you, Mr. Fielding!

PAUL: How's the filing? Keeping busy?

TRIXIE: As always!

> *(Trixie pulls the paper out of her typewriter, wads it up, and throws it into the trashcan.)*

PAUL: You throw away the work of twelve people, Trixie. I don't know what we would do without you.

TRIXIE: Flatterer.

PAUL: Is Max in yet?

TRIXIE: No. *(MAX MARSHALL storms into the office.)* Yes. *(He walks directly past them without pausing to say hello, and goes into his office.)* No. *(Max comes out with a newspaper in his hand, opens his mouth like he wants to say something.)* Yes. *(He stops himself. Goes back into his office.)* No. *(Max comes back out, frustrated.)* Maybe…?

MAX: How can you just stand there?

PAUL: Practice. It takes some doing, but eventually most people catch on.

MAX: That's not what I—! Did you see this?

> *(Max shakes the newspaper.)*

PAUL: Before or after you began shaking it at us?

> *(Max brings it over to Trixie's desk and spreads it out.)*

MAX: THERE! Right there!

TRIXIE: Two for one girdles at Woolworths?

PAUL: I've always thought you cut a rather dashing figure myself.

MAX: Would you two stop! THERE! Palladino Architects just received the commission for the new city hall. Why didn't we hear about this project?!

TRIXIE: We did.

MAX: What?

(Trixie jogs over to the filing cabinet and digs around for the letter.)

TRIXIE: Sure! We got a letter. I filed it for you.

MAX: You what?!

TRIXIE: You kept telling me I wasn't keeping up with the filing so I decided to surprise you. SURPRISE!

(She holds up the letter triumphantly. Max is defeated.)

MAX: TRIXIE! Do you know how big a commission this would have been?

PAUL: Now, now. No use crying over spilled cement.

MAX: We're broke, Paul.

PAUL: We're always broke, Max.

MAX: Well, this time is different.

PAUL: It is always darkest before the dawn.

MAX: Or after sunset when we haven't paid the electric bill.

PAUL: Did you pay this month's electric bill?

TRIXIE: I decided to buy coffee instead.

PAUL: Excellent choice.

MAX: How can you two not comprehend the gravity of what I'm saying? Trixie! TRIXIE I can understand. But you, Paul. YOU! We've known each other since university! We're on the brink of ruin and you two are making jokes!

PAUL: I don't think we were joking about the coffee.

TRIXIE: I wasn't.

MAX: That is it! This is the end of free coffee! If you want a cup of free coffee, you are going to put a nickel in this jar!

>   (*He empties a jar full of pencils.*)

TRIXIE: A nickel in the jar?

MAX: Yes! A nickel in the jar! Like so!

>   (*He takes a nickel from his pocket and triumphantly puts it in.*)

TRIXIE: Like so?

MAX: Like so.

TRIXIE: And then you pour yourself a cup of coffee?

(She pours herself a cup of coffee.)

MAX: Yes! You pour yourself a cup of coffee.

TRIXIE: Like so?

MAX: Yes, like so.

(She hands the cup of coffee to Paul.)

TRIXIE: Well, that seems easy enough. But what if I only had a quarter?

MAX: It is the same principal! You put a quarter in the kitty…

(He takes a quarter from his pocket and demonstrates)

TRIXIE: Like so… then you pour yourself a cup of coffee! Like so. Then take all the change. Like so!

(In one motion, she pours another cup of coffee, dumps all the money in the coffee kitty into her open purse sitting on her desk, then merrily clinks glasses with Paul before she sits down at her desk to drink.)

MAX: I—! We owe the bank seven thousand dollars by the end of the week or it's over!

PAUL: Max, we're not doing this. I warned you.

MAX: Don't!

PAUL: You decided to take that dame down to Rio rather than bid for the Henderson job.

MAX: Don't throw that back at me.

PAUL: I'm not fixing this for you. AGAIN. You said that YOU, and I quote, had it all under control and that I, and I quote, worried too much.

MAX: How was I supposed to know it'd be the only opportunity since October?!

PAUL: That's your job! You're the president!

MAX: You're my partner!

PAUL: I'm just supposed to design the buildings!

MAX: I know. I KNOW! I just didn't---KNOW! Paaaaaul... I thought she loved me, Paul. I thought... but she didn't...and now... OH Paul... If I have to call my father and tell him I ruined his company...

PAUL: Chin up. Sure pickings have been slim since your pop retired, but we're still new. Business will build.

TRIXIE: It's like your father always said, "You've always been a little slow."

MAX: When we took over this firm, Paul, I swore... I swore I would show him I could be a success...

6

TRIXIE: Mr. Marshall did run an excellent firm.

MAX: I know.

TRIXIE: We were busy all the time with him at the helm.

MAX: I. Know.

TRIXIE: It's funny how people don't even seem to know we exist since you took over.

MAX: I KNOW!

PAUL: Max, take a deep breath.

MAX: I'm drowning.

PAUL: We're not underwater yet.

MAX: The walls are closing in!

PAUL: Max, we're architects. If the walls close in, it's going to be very bad for business.

MAX: I'M A FAILURE! PAUL! I can't let it end like this! We have GOT to land something! We'll just… we'll economize. No more coffee! No more buying supplies! We'll stop paying our bills.

TRIXIE: We already did.

MAX: What? *(Trixie drops a tall stack of bills in front of Max.)* Why didn't you give these to me earlier?

TRIXIE: I didn't want to ruin your day.

(Max walks over to the window and looks down.)

MAX: How high up are we?

PAUL: 3rd floor. You'd just break your legs. Trixie? Where are those job requests you so efficiently put away?

TRIXIE: Over there! *(She points at the filing cabinets. Paul jogs over.)* I filed them under "G".

PAUL: "G"?

TRIXIE: "Give these to Max".

PAUL: Makes perfect sense.

MAX: I can't breathe.

PAUL: Here they are! A whole pile of design requests.

TRIXIE: And you said I wasn't organized.

MAX: We wouldn't happen to have any rat poison lying about, would we?

TRIXIE: Sure! Next to the soap powder.

(Max gets up and goes into the other room.)

PAUL: Well, a couple of these are out of date. *(Paul dumps a huge pile in the wastebasket.)* MAX! I think we might have found something!

(Max comes in with a coffee cup in one hand and the box of rat poison in the other.)

MAX: What?

PAUL: Put that down. You're not killing yourself today.

MAX: I wasn't planning on it.

TRIXIE: You found my cup!

PAUL: And you're not killing Trixie, either. Come on, Max! I found the solution to our problems. Look! A private retirement home is being built for the hard working veterans of this proud city's police force!

MAX: A retirement home?

PAUL: Right there in black and white for our boys in blue.

MAX: I had no idea!

TRIXIE: Well, you would if you looked at the mail I file for you.

MAX: Oh, Trixie! I could kiss you!

TRIXIE: Okay!

MAX: Right here! We have the request right here! This job was meant for us! Paul, you work up the initial design and I'll let them know we're definitely in.

PAUL: Already on it!

> *(Paul leaps over to the drafting table and gets a blank piece of paper.)*

MAX: We'll have to keep costs low, but I'm sure with some smart contracting... If only we knew someone on the building commission...

TRIXIE: You mean, like, someone who is intimately involved with this project?

MAX: Yes.

TRIXIE: Like someone with deep pockets who might be able to influence the decision making process?

MAX: Yes!

TRIXIE: Like someone who might be a close personal friend to someone who works right here at TF Architects?

MAX: YES! Do you know someone?

TRIXIE: No.

MAX: Right.

TRIXIE: But maybe someone does at the Ladies' Auxiliary Retirement Home Afternoon Fundraiser Tea.

> (*Trixie holds up an invitation. Max rips it out of her hand, devouring the words. He looks at Trixie in delight.*)

MAX: GWEN!

TRIXIE: (*pointing to herself*) Trixie.

MAX: No, GWEN!

TRIXIE: I'm pretty sure it's Trixie, but I've been wrong before.

MAX: Not you. Gwen Gladwell!

PAUL: Who's Gwen Gladwell?

MAX: Old friend… of a friend. She is the chair of this fundraiser. If somehow I can rekindle our acquaintance… convince her I'm the man for her job…

PAUL: Maaax…Is your pitch going to be focused on the "job" or the "rekindle" integer of this equation?

MAX: Whatever it takes to keep this company afloat.

PAUL: Max…?

MAX: We were just friends.

PAUL: MAX….

MAX: Okay, a little more.

PAUL: The last time you let love guide TF Architecture, you made the Titanic look like a leaky rowboat.

MAX: This time will be different…

PAUL: It is ALWAYS "different".

MAX: Gwen is different.

PAUL: You say that every time.

MAX: Paul? It is all under control. Trust me! Things are looking brighter already!

(The electricity goes out.)

TRIXIE: Anyone want coffee?

(END OF SCENE)

ACT I

Scene 2

Morning in the office the next day. Trixie hums to herself as she gets a cup of coffee. She puts a quarter into the coffee kitty, then pours all of the change into her purse. She takes a triumphant sip. Max storms in, but this time with a spring in his step.

MAX: Paul! PAUL! Where are you Paul?

TRIXIE: You'll need to shout louder.

MAX: What?

TRIXIE: He's still at home.

MAX: Why isn't he here? I have such news! Such news!

TRIXIE: What news?

MAX: It is a secret.

TRIXIE: What's a secret?

MAX: I have wooed the mighty Gwen Gladwell! My prowess is invincible!

TRIXIE: That IS the best kept secret in town.

MAX: Just… tell Paul as soon as he gets in that I want to meet with him. I want to surprise Gwen Gladwell with our plans this afternoon, so we have two hours to get all our ducks in a row.

TRIXIE: Might be easier to carry them in a basket.

MAX: What?

TRIXIE: The ducks.

MAX: There are no actual ducks associated with this project…

TRIXIE: Are you sure? Because I'd definitely hire the man who brought me a basket of widdle duckwings.

MAX: Just… Tell Paul we have a two-hour meeting.

TRIXIE: Sure thing, Max.

MAX: No. You know what? Starting today, it's Mr. Marshall.

TRIXIE: Where? I should put on some coffee.

MAX: No, I'm Mr. Marshall.

TRIXIE: Excuse me, but I worked for Mr. Marshall and you are not Mr. Marshall.

MAX: Yes, I am.

TRIXIE: He's your father.

MAX: It is also my name.

TRIXIE: Nooooo…. you're his son. Max.

MAX: I just… I want you to call me Mister— Never mind. Where's Paul?

TRIXIE: He's in a meeting with you.

MAX: No, he isn't.

TRIXIE: You just said he has a two-hour meeting with you.

MAX: Yes. But not yet… I mean… why isn't he here?

TRIXIE: I don't know. Did you tell him about the meeting?

MAX: Not yet.

TRIXIE: Well, there's your problem…

MAX: THAT'S WHAT I'M TRYING TO DO!

TRIXIE: I'm just saying that if you want to hold a secret meeting, maybe you should tell the person you want to come about the secret meeting. But what do I know. I just buy the coffee.

MAX: Can't you... Fine. FINE! I'll just... FINE!

(Max goes into his office and Paul comes in. He throws his hat on the hat rack.)

PAUL: Good morning, Trixie!

TRIXIE: Good morning, Paul!

PAUL: How are things this glorious day?

TRIXIE: Fine and dandy!

PAUL: Sweeter than candy! What messages do you have for me?

TRIXIE: Max has a two-hour meeting. I'd tell you more, but it's a secret.

PAUL: What's a secret?

TRIXIE: Something you don't tell anybody.

PAUL: If you had a secret you weren't going to tell me, what would it be?

TRIXIE: That things went very well with Gwen Gladwell.

PAUL: That's swell news, Trixie!

TRIXIE: It's a secret, though, so keep it under your hat.

PAUL: Mum's the word. How's Max this morning?

TRIXIE: He seems very distracted. I think his father is coming in.

PAUL: Then we must keep our heads low and our coffee cups lower.

> *(Paul disappears into the kitchen. GWEN GLADWELL enters.)*

TRIXIE: May I help you?

GWEN: Yes. My name is Miss. Gladwell. I'm supposed to have a meeting later, but wanted to see if Mr. Marshall was available for lunch?

TRIXIE: Oh, he doesn't work here anymore.

GWEN: Oh! I'm sorry! He gave me this business address. Do you know where I might find him?

TRIXIE: Ummm...

> *(Paul re-enters. There is a lightning bolt of attraction between him and Gwen.)*

PAUL: Why, hello! May I help you?

GWEN: Hello. I'm trying to find Max Marshall.

TRIXIE: OH! MAX! I thought you meant his father— (*Paul pushes her.*) PAUL!

GWEN: His father "Paul"?

PAUL: Yes. His father "Paul".

TRIXIE: I thought his first name was "mister".

PAUL: It is. Now, be a dear and percolate a new pot for Mr. Marshall, would you, Trixie?

TRIXIE: Sure thing! You got a nickel?

PAUL: (*taking a fist full of coins from his pocket*) I'm buying our entire stock. Brew it all! (*he pushes her into the kitchen*) Now, let's see… MAX. Max… Max…

GWEN: Yes, Max Marshall? The owner of this firm, I believe?

PAUL: Oh… HIM. Yes. So, you're here to… see him?

GWEN: Yes. Do you know where I can find him? I need to talk to him about the police retirement home?

PAUL: Yes. Absolutely! I've been working on it all week.

GWEN: Really? I only spoke with Max yesterday.

PAUL: We are passionate about your project. Just... passionate. You know... I do all of the... design work... for our firm.

GWEN: Really.

PAUL: My name is Paul. I'm the lead architect. Max is more of our paperwork and finances man.

GWEN: Or, as some might say, the president.

PAUL: That, too. Listen, we're getting started on the wrong foot...

GWEN: How many feet do you have, because I think you've run out.

PAUL: Max is in a meeting for the next two hours. Why don't you let me buy you a cup of coffee until he gets out?

GWEN: What on earth for?

PAUL: To make up for me being such a heel. Having the most beautiful woman in the world walk through the door got me all flummoxed.

GWEN: Flattery will get you everywhere. No funny stuff?

PAUL: Scouts honor!

GWEN: I've got twenty-five cents that says you never were a scout.

PAUL: Would you like to see my merit badge in chemistry?

GWEN: I can already see you earned it in inventing.

PAUL: Such mistrust!

GWEN: Come along, little boy. Let's get that coffee so your mouth can do something besides talk.

PAUL: You have a very lovely mouth... the way your lips just curve like two flying buttresses...

GWEN: Buttresses?

PAUL: Coming from an architect? That is the highest compliment I can dish out.

GWEN: Now listen here, Mister Frank Lloyd Wrong, I might let you take me out to coffee, but touch these buttresses and you're going to be the one in need of some structural support.

(Gwen and Paul exit. Trixie enters with the coffee pot. Max comes out of his office, arms filled with messy paperwork.)

MAX: Trixie, did you do any of the filing I asked you to do when I left yesterday?

TRIXIE: No. You left.

MAX: What?

TRIXIE: I figured the office was closed.

MAX: I left at 2PM!

TRIXIE: And I appreciate having the afternoon off.

MAX: Argh! Is Paul in yet?

TRIXIE: In where?

MAX: In here.

TRIXIE: Well, if he is, you better get him out. He's supposed to be in a meeting with you.

MAX: I know he's supposed to be in a meeting with me.

TRIXIE: Well if you knew that, why are you here? Tsk. You'd think I had nothing better to do than answer silly questions.

MAX: But he's not in the meeting with me.

TRIXIE: Of course he's not. You're in here instead of your office where the meeting is taking place. It seems rather rude to stand him up for a meeting which you called, if you ask me.

MAX: But he's the one who stood me up.

TRIXIE: He stood you up? Well, you can sit down if you like. *(Trixie motions to the guest chair and, without thinking, Max starts to sit down.)* But frankly, I like you so much better standing. You cut quite a striking figure in that suit.

MAX: Please do not comment on my suit. Or my figure. I am simply trying to find Paul.

TRIXIE: Well, if you would listen for one minute you'd know that's what I've been trying to tell you. He's not here.

MAX: But where did he go?

TRIXIE: How should I know? You're the one who lost him.

MAX: I need to find him.

TRIXIE: Well, my Aunt Betsy said that whenever you lose someone, you should think back to where you saw them last…

MAX: But I haven't seen him at all.

TRIXIE: Not at all?

MAX: No!

TRIXIE: Oh dear! Should I call a doctor?

MAX: What? Why?

TRIXIE: The sudden onset of blindness is a very serious situation.

MAX: What? There has been no sudden... onset...

TRIXIE: You mean after all these years... you've been pretending to see Paul? Pretending to see me? Oh! I could just cry! Oh, poor Mr. Max!

MAX: Don't cry.

TRIXIE: You are so brave!

MAX: I am not brave.

TRIXIE: Yes you are!

MAX: I can see you just fine.

TRIXIE: You do not have to shoulder this burden alone!

MAX: I'm not shouldering anything...

TRIXIE: Don't you worry, Mr. Max. Your secret is safe with me. Lots of famous men are blind… Louis Braille, Willie Johnson, Helen Keller…

MAX: Helen Keller is not a man.

TRIXIE: Oh, Mr. Max! So blind, you don't even know the difference between a man and a woman.

MAX: I am quite aware of the differences of a man and a woman.

> *(Trixie wraps herself around Max, taking his hands and placing them on her body.)*

TRIXIE: Here! Stand close to me! Feel my face. I sacrifice my honor for your education!

MAX: Miss Fuller! Please!

TRIXIE: Wrap your arms around me and let me lead you through the office like a seeing-eye dog.

MAX: I can see you just fine.

TRIXIE: Stop pretending!

MAX: I can see you!

TRIXIE: If you can see me, tell me what I look like.

MAX: Well, you are an average woman of average height…

TRIXIE: Blind as a bat!

MAX: I am not!

TRIXIE: If you can see, tell me what color my eyes are.

(Max steps closer and Trixie gazes up at him.)

MAX: Well, they are a rather lovely bluish color.

TRIXIE: Why, Max! *(Trixie slaps Max.)* How dare you!

MAX: What?

TRIXIE: Tricking me! Pretending you were blind when you were not! Was this a ploy to get fresh? Taking advantage of a poor secretary?

MAX: I assure you, that was not my intent…

TRIXIE: What do you call that holding me close, like this. And feeling my face with your fingers, like this, and gazing down into my eyes?

MAX: That was you!

TRIXIE: Me? How dare you! You owe me an apology.

MAX: Of course.

TRIXIE: I'll get my hat.

> *(Trixie gets up and gets her purse and hat, as well as Max's hat.)*

MAX: Why?

TRIXIE: Because you're taking me to lunch to apologize.

MAX: Lunch?

TRIXIE: Really, Max, if you wanted to ask me out, you should have just asked. There was no need for these silly games.

> *(Trixie puts Max's hat on his head.)*

MAX: I didn't plan…

TRIXIE: This wasn't planned? Why, would you look at you. You are so impulsive and romantic.

MAX: I really must speak with Paul.

> *(Trixie slips her arm into Max's and walks him out of the office.)*

TRIXIE: Well, aren't we in luck! Paul is in a meeting right now which will last at least two hours, so we will have plenty of time before he gets back.

MAX: But that meeting was with me...

(END OF SCENE)

ACT I

Scene 3

Lights come up on a cafe. Paul and Gwen are sitting at a table. On the wall is a chalkboard touting the day's menu specials.

PAUL: So how did a smart woman like yourself get talked into raising all the funds for the new policemen's retirement center?

GWEN: Aside from my father being the police commissioner...?

PAUL: Boy, I just stepped in it. I just meant---

GWEN: Really, if I had known what I was in for, I would have taken up a nice, quiet career in an asylum.

PAUL: The joys of civil service...

GWEN: It's important, though. It's my father's dream to take care of the good men on his force, the men who can barely make ends meet, yet refuse to take a bribe. I swear his department is the only one not bankrolled by some crooked politician... or... or... organized crime.

What he's been through to restore this city's trust.. He's more important to me than any man I know... well... except, Max is rather special too, isn't he?

PAUL: Max?

GWEN: Yes.

PAUL: Oh, he's a fine enough fellow…

GWEN: Yes, he is.

PAUL: When you first meet him.

GWEN: I've known him since high school.

PAUL: Sometimes it takes awhile to get to know a person.

GWEN: And how long have you known him?

PAUL: Oh… we went to university together. We apprenticed for his father and then Max took over the company a few months ago. How about you? Were you close? The two of you?

GWEN: Come out and ask it, Twinkle Toes.

PAUL: Ask what?

GWEN: The question you keep dancing around.

PAUL: I have no idea what you mean.

GWEN: "Were we an item?"

PAUL: Why, I would never be so forward! Such intimacies are a private affair! Really. But since you brought it up, were you? An item?

GWEN: Yes. We went steady.

PAUL: Max.

GWEN: Yes.

PAUL: And you?

GWEN: Yes.

PAUL: Why?

GWEN: You may find this hard to believe, but I liked him. Very much.

PAUL: Very much?

GWEN: Very much.

PAUL: He said that you were a friend of a friend.

GWEN: I wouldn't expect a man like you to understand.

PAUL: I understand Max.

GWEN: Well, I do, too.

PAUL: I don't think you do.

GWEN: The way he tracked me down. After all these years.

PAUL: Listen, Gwen, don't take Max showing up out of the blue for more than it is.

GWEN: You're just jealous.

PAUL: Jealous?

GWEN: Jealous.

PAUL: Such mistrust!

GWEN: If it quacks like a duck.

PAUL: So what does Max quack like?

GWEN: Like a romantic.

PAUL: A romantic duck...?

GWEN: I'm not surprised at all he didn't tell you about us.

PAUL: Why?

GWEN: You seem like the type to look at our connection as an invitation to crash the party.

PAUL: I've never so much as cut in on a lindy hop.

GWEN: How refreshing.

PAUL: I have no horse in this race.

GWEN: You seem to have no issue sizing up the fillies.

PAUL: Max is my best friend and I try to look out for him. Despite himself.

GWEN: Oh? So this is all about protecting poor defenseless Max.

PAUL: Yes.

GWEN: Really.

PAUL: You don't believe me.

GWEN: Quack. Quack.

(Max and Trixie enter.)

MAX: Is that Paul?

TRIXIE: Of course not, silly. He's in a meeting with you.

MAX: Paul! You're supposed to be in a meeting with me!

PAUL: I was… but you were in a meeting, so I came here! Fancy that!

GWEN: You told me he was in a meeting for two hours.

TRIXIE: He is. With Paul. But he stood Paul up.

(Max notices Gwen and is immediately all apologies.)

MAX: I did not. I did not!

TRIXIE: And yet here we are. If you had gone to your meeting, none of us would be here. Tsk. For shame.

PAUL: I couldn't have said it better, Trixie.

MAX: This is not what it seems!

GWEN: What? That you are out to lunch with another woman?

TRIXIE: Oh, I'm not the other woman. I'm his fiancé.

MAX: No, you're not.

TRIXIE: He just doesn't know it yet.

MAX: No, she's not!

GWEN: So, I guess that makes ME the other woman.

PAUL: I tried to warn you.

MAX: This has all been a big misunderstanding.

GWEN: And here I was going to hand over the police retirement building on a silver platter.

MAX & PAUL: You WHAT?!

GWEN: Oh, now you are all business.

PAUL: There is a time for work and a time for play.

MAX: And right now, we work.

TRIXIE: I should be taking notes.

> *(Trixie wipes the "Specials" menu clean and grabs a piece of chalk.)*

GWEN: Yes, I pulled every string I could and you two have the opportunity to present your design to my father.

MAX: And then to the building commission…?

GWEN: He IS the building commission.

MAX & PAUL: We have a job! We have a job!

> *(Trixie writes "Job" on the specials board.)*

GWEN: You don't have the job yet!

MAX & PAUL: We might have a job! We might have a job!

(Trixie crosses out "Job" on the specials board.)

GWEN: Boys!

PAUL: Oh, Gwen! I could just kiss you!

MAX: What?

PAUL: Merely an expression of speech.

MAX: Now, is there any possibility of any sort of retainer fee..?

GWEN: You want a retainer… before you've even presented for the job?

MAX: Never hurts to ask.

GWEN: I suppose I could spot you something. How much do you need?

MAX: Seven… thousand…

GWEN: That's quite a lot…

PAUL: What a joker! Retainer fee… why, next he's going to start saying he makes his workers buy their own coffee. Gwen, this is jim dandy. We will have the design for you by next week and you can tell that commission of yours we are going to knock their socks off! Thank you!

GWEN: You're welcome. Anything to help Max.

PAUL: Now. There is work to be done!

GWEN: You're right. I really should be going.

(Max and Paul rush over to pull out Gwen's chair and skirmish over it. It drops on Max's toe.)

PAUL: I'll walk you to the door. Pick up the check, would you, Max? For our new client?

(Paul walks Gwen out of the restaurant, leaving Max holding the chair. Trixie sits down in it as if Max pulled it out for her.)

MAX: Do you have any money?

(Trixie opens up her pocket book and dumps out all the change she's been taking from the kitty onto the table.)

TRIXIE: You should drink more coffee.

(Paul comes back.)

PAUL: MAX! We are in business. We are in business!

MAX: Nooo… this is not better. This is not better!

PAUL: What are you talking about? We are presenting to her father!

MAX: We are not going to be in business long enough to make the presentation. I can't believe I thought we could get this wrapped up before the bank's deadline. Gwen never went fast.

PAUL: You'll get us an extension.

MAX: We need the money now! How much is my life insurance policy?

TRIXIE: Two grand.

PAUL: But it is null and void if you commit suicide.

MAX: How much is her life insurance policy?

TRIXIE: Six grand.

PAUL: But it does not cover murder.

MAX: We are this close. THIS CLOSE! We're doomed. DOOMED!

> (*RUBY DELEONI*, *a va-va-va-voom woman, enters and listens with interest.*)

TRIXIE: What you need is someone with deep pockets.

MAX: Yes.

TRIXIE: Who is looking for investment potential.

MAX: Yes!

TRIXIE: Who sees this enterprise as not just a business, but an opportunity to create a lasting monument.

MAX: YES! Do you know anyone?

TRIXIE: No.

MAX: ARGH!

PAUL: Come on, Trixie. Let Max figure this out. There is work to be done!

> *(Paul and Trixie exit. Ruby Deleoni sidles over with a flask and pours Max a drink.)*

RUBY: Why you looking so glum, chum?

MAX: What? Oh! Hello.

RUBY: I haven't seen a face that down since my ex lost his bootlegger.

MAX: It's nothing. Just some... a business matter.

RUBY: Business, huh? I always had a head for numbers.

MAX: Really?

RUBY: Scout's honor.

MAX: You were a girl scout?

RUBY: I was always more of a boy scout. Now tell Miss Ruby your troubles and see if she can't come up with a nice, easy solution.

MAX: I owe a bank $7000.

RUBY: Is that all?

MAX: Is that…all?

RUBY: Oh sweetie, you hang out with Ruby and seven-grand is chump change.

MAX: You know any chumps?

RUBY: Maybe one. Listen, I got a cousin that likes to make loans. A real butter and eggs man.

MAX: I don't have any collateral.

RUBY: Doesn't matter. This cousin of mine? He's family. A friend of mine is a friend of theirs.

MAX: I like your family.

RUBY: And my family is going to love you. Don't you worry. We loan money to people we believe in.

> *(Ruby continues to pour drinks as Max becomes increasingly drunk and tries to turn on the charm.)*

MAX: You can believe in me. I'm very believable!

RUBY: Sure you are, honey.

MAX: Would your family be interested in investing in architecture?

RUBY: We value loyalty over money.

MAX: I can do loyal! Call your cousin!

RUBY: Of course, we charge interest.

MAX: Naturally.

RUBY: How big a project are we talking here?

MAX: Big. I mean… not enormous, but a reasonable size proportionate to our firm.

RUBY: And what monument to man is your firm building?

MAX: A retirement home. For police officers.

RUBY: *(laughing)* Are you telling me you need money to build a retirement home for our city's finest?

MAX: Yes.

RUBY: Oooh, my friend... Wouldn't you know I have been looking for a way to pay back the police commissioner for his years of sterling service. I can't wait to get waist deep in this project.

MAX: Waist... deep...

RUBY: Listen, I'm going to send my nephew over...

MAX: I thought he was your cousin.

RUBY: Same difference. Listen, he'll bring the $7000 AND, because I like you, he himself is a contractor and provides some of the lowest prices in town.

MAX: Does he have any experience constructing large buildings?

RUBY: You're gonna love him. He's tops with concrete and has only the best connections.

MAX: I... I am overwhelmed. Are you an angel?

RUBY: Sent from heaven above.

MAX: Can I ever see you again?

RUBY: Oh don't you worry. I am going to make sure to provide some very hands on project management.

MAX: Lovely! That would be lovely! Thank you!

RUBY: Sure thing, kid. I have a feeling this is going to be a very profitable enterprise for all parties involved.

(END OF SCENE)

Act I

Scene 4

Morning the next day. Trixie is manning the office when a shady looking man, VITO DELEONI, in a sharp suit and fedora comes in. He looks around the room.

TRIXIE: Hello?

VITO: Is this TF Architecture?

TRIXIE: Sure is! Want some coffee?

VITO: Sure, toots.

TRIXIE: You'll need to give me a nickel.

VITO: You know, I have here a loan from my boss to your boss. What do you say you put that nickel against the money he is about to owe me.

TRIXIE: Against the money he owes you?

VITO: Sure! Listen, Max Marshall is about to borrow money from my boss, right?

TRIXIE: Right.

VITO: So everything you buy technically belongs to us until he pays it back.

TRIXIE: Right.

VITO: So every cup of coffee you drink is taking money away from our investment.

TRIXIE: Right!

VITO: So, in actuality, he owes me for every cup of coffee I drink. Plus interest.

TRIXIE: That makes complete sense! But what about if I drink a cup of coffee?

VITO: You? You, pretty lady, should never have to buy a drink ever. Consider yourself from here on out a personal guest of myself.

TRIXIE: Oh… You're so generous…

VITO: Put it on Max's tab.

TRIXIE: Okay!

(*Trixie pours Vito and herself a cup of coffee.*)

VITO: I hear that Max Marshall is gonna have a job for some contractors.

TRIXIE: We're hoping to build the retirement home for the police commissioner.

VITO: No kidding. That's aces.

TRIXIE: But with cash flow, we're gonna have to do it really cheap. I heard Max say we're going to have to rob a man named Peter in order to pay Paul.

VITO: Don't you worry about that, little lady. We're experts at getting Paul his bread.

TRIXIE: Oh, I already made him a sandwich.

VITO: What?

TRIXIE: What?

VITO: Listen, my boys and me? We're gonna make sure that all expenses are spared on this special project. In fact, I bet a bunch of my guys are gonna volunteer to do this job for free.

TRIXIE: Boy, I like you. I have a way of telling about people.

VITO: What can I say? I'm a stand up kind of guy.

(*Trixie motions to the guest chair.*)

TRIXIE: Really? Because it's okay if you want to sit down.

VITO: No. I'm good standing.

(Trixie continues motioning to the guest chair.)

TRIXIE: But if you wanted, you could.

VITO: I could. But I don't want to.

(Trixie continues motioning to the chair, distressed he won't sit.)

TRIXIE: Well, I want what you want.

VITO: You're a good girl, toots. Listen. Speakin' of wants, I have this list of things that would make doing this job so much easier. Think you can get these for me?

(He hands her a list.)

TRIXIE: Sure! Ooo… Dempsey dumpsters?

VITO: Waste management. We like to keep a clean construction site.

TRIXIE: Should I wait to place this order until after we give you the contract?

VITO: No.

TRIXIE: Okay!

VITO: Is that boss of yours in?

TRIXIE: He's in his office. I'd get him for you, but he's really angry.

VITO: What's he so angry about?

TRIXIE: Oh, people and money. He hates debts.

VITO: My kind of people.

TRIXIE: You, too, huh?

VITO: I'll have to let him know I'm happy to help him settle his debts, too.

TRIXIE: You really are a full service contractor, aren't you?

VITO: It is the Deleoni way.

(Trixie giggles as Max enters.)

MAX: Trixie! Oh! Hello. Mr. Deleoni? I didn't expect to see you so soon.

VITO: I'm all about punctuality.

MAX: Good! Good. I like that.

VITO: So, you're the man with the job.

MAX: I am. We have a big job. We need a true professional.

VITO: Professional is my middle name.

TRIXIE: Really?

MAX: (*sighing*) Noooo...

VITO: Now, don't you be talking to this charming young dame like that!

MAX: Apologies. We have a relationship...

> (*Max goes to pour himself a cup of coffee.*)

TRIXIE: Aw, Max....

MAX: Working... relationship... (*Trixie clears her throat reminding Max to put a nickel in the coffee kitty.*) So. Mr. Deleoni. As soon as we sign the contract, we hope to break ground right away. I hear you have worked with concrete?

VITO: We're keen with concrete. We specialize in business management, waste disposal, concrete, and shoes.

TRIXIE: Ooo!

MAX: That sounds wonderful! And I understand that you have a loan for me.

(Vito pulls a stack of cash from his pocket.)

VITO: Here you go!

MAX: Oh my! Shouldn't I sign something…

VITO: Let's just say we are gentlemen, and a handshake between gentlemen is all that two refined men like you and me should ever need. If for some reason you don't fulfill the expectations of our business relationship, we'll just settle this. As gentlemen.

MAX: This is wonderful. Wonderful! Well. Put 'er there, Mr. Deleoni! It is a pleasure doing business with you!

VITO: And with you!

MAX: As soon as we get everything finalized, I'll be in touch to find out what you need to move forward.

VITO: I left a list with your secretary so she can get right on it. Even gave her the relational discount.

MAX: Such efficiency!

VITO: Listen, our goal is to make sure that from here on out, we're the only contractors you ever work with.

MAX: I like you already!

VITO: Hey! We're family!

MAX: Family!

(Vito gives Trixie a wink, and walks out the door. Max dances around the room.)

MAX: Oh, Trixie! Things are looking up! It is a great, big beautiful day! Trixie, I need you to take a memo.

TRIXIE: Which one?

MAX: What do you mean?

TRIXIE: I have lots memos all over my desk. Which one would you like for me to take?

MAX: No, I am going to dictate a memo to you and you will type it up for me.

TRIXIE: Sure! You can get me a cup of coffee.

MAX: What?

TRIXIE: If I'm going to type a memo for you, you could at least buy me a cup of coffee. Typing is a valuable service.

MAX: I'm already paying you for your service. I'm your boss.

TRIXIE: I thought you were my friend.

MAX: I am your friend.

TRIXIE: Oh! I would never charge a friend to type a memo. You can just buy me a cup of coffee.

MAX: FINE! I'll buy you a cup of coffee.

TRIXIE: Oh lovely. All right, what would you like me to type?

MAX: "To Smith & Sons Bank. "

TRIXIE: Oh, there seems to be something wrong with my typewriter.

MAX: What?

TRIXIE: The keys keep sticking. Here, see if you can figure out what's wrong. *(Max sits down)* Try typing "To Smith & Sons Bank."

MAX: *(types)* It's fine.

TRIXIE: Well, try typing some more.

  (Paul enters)

MAX: "I am pleased to enclose payment against our outstanding balance. Signed, Max Marshall."

PAUL: Max, why are you typing that?

MAX: What? Oh! Trixie! Type that!

TRIXIE: Look! Someone already did!

PAUL: No, Max, what I mean is why are you typing that. We don't have the money to pay back the bank.

MAX: Mitt me kid! I got us the money!

(Paul rushes over to shake Max's hand.)

PAUL: You did? No kidding?

MAX: AND they put me in touch with a cut rate contractor who is going to save us so much, we can buy steak for dinner!

PAUL: Max! I KNEW you had it in you!

MAX: That'll teach my old man. I feel like celebrating!

PAUL: Now, we don't have Gwen's job yet…

MAX: It's in the can!

PAUL: Where did you get this money?

MAX: Oh… I simply worked the ol' Marshall charm on a lonely woman looking for an investment opportunity…

PAUL: Oh Max…

MAX: What?

PAUL: Not again…

MAX: It's fine!

PAUL: You got the money to do a project for your old flame by wooing the wallet of another woman?

MAX: I got us the money, didn't I?

PAUL: Max…

MAX: Stop it, Paul. Stop. Opportunity knocked and I, unlike you, answered the door. I've got this all under control.

> *(Max leans against the drafting table. It flips and he falls to the ground.)*

> (END OF SCENE)

Act I

Scene 5

Mid-morning the following week. Gwen and Max enter the office of TF Architecture. Trixie sits at her desk finishing her cup of coffee.

GWEN: Oh, Max. You were simply marvelous! You couldn't have impressed my father more!

MAX: Trixie? Could you get us some coffee?

TRIXIE: We're out.

MAX: Out?

TRIXIE: Someone drank it all.

MAX: Well, what do you say about heading down to the shop and picking us up some more?

TRIXIE: There's no money in the coffee kitty.

MAX: Coffee kitty! What an imagination! *(Max drops the coffee kitty into the trash. He peels off a couple dollar bills from his bank roll and hands them to Trixie, trying to*

impress Gwen.) We... don't... make our... employees...
Be a dear, would you, and go get us two cups?

TRIXIE: Sure, darling. What would you like in them,
sugar?

MAX: Yes.

TRIXIE: What, sugar?

MAX: Yes.

TRIXIE: No. What would you like in them?

MAX: Sugar.

TRIXIE: Yes, dear?

MAX: Two black coffees.

TRIXIE: Right-o!

   (Trixie leaves.)

MAX: This is all so wonderful, Gwen! YOU are so
wonderful!

GWEN: My father is over the moon with how ready
you are to move forward! It's like you were always Mr.
Right. For the job.

MAX: Oh, we started throwing ideas around the
moment we heard about this project. Not for the

money or anything. Just because we thought it would be so fantastic! To build a retirement home! For police officers!

GWEN: The Gladwell House. My father's name right over the door. It will be his legacy and people will *always* associate it with him. And you made it happen.

MAX: Me? You're right. Me. Oh, Gwen. Can I show you a special idea I've been working on?

GWEN: Yes!

MAX: You wait right there. Don't you move a muscle! Not a pretty little muscle!

> *(In unison, Max goes into his office to get his blueprints, Paul comes out of his office with an armful of permits, and Trixie re-enters with two paper coffee cups.)*

PAUL: Trixie! It is like you read my mind.

TRIXIE: One for you. And one for you.

> *(Gwen and Paul take their cups.)*

PAUL: How did the presentation go?

GWEN: I stand here the proud bearer of a contract binding the firm of TF Architecture to the new police retirement center!

PAUL: Oh Gwen! This is marvelous!

GWEN: It was a marvelous design.

PAUL: Flattery will get you everywhere.

GWEN: Max already signed. All we need is yours right here, "partner." Say, what does the TF stand for?

PAUL: Trixie Fuller.

GWEN: How did she manage that?

TRIXIE: Manage what?

GWEN: Getting two men to name their architecture firm after you?

PAUL: When we took over the company, the paperwork said "name", so she put in her name. And that is why Max makes me do all the paperwork now.

TRIXIE: Funny how that worked out.

PAUL: Speaking of which, here are all those permits to be filed, filled out with love by yours truly.

GWEN: So, you just left it at TF? You didn't make her change it?

TRIXIE: (*she picks up her nail buffer*) We got busy.

GWEN: Really.

TRIXIE: Sorry. I'm busy.

PAUL: And that's how she did it.

GWEN: And you didn't fire her?

PAUL: You think we haven't tried? Trixie! You're fired!

TRIXIE: I'll get right on that, boss!

PAUL: Like invading Russia in winter... Listen, Gwen, let's hit the Grove Hotel tonight to celebrate! They've got that swell new supper club.

GWEN: I really shouldn't. Max and I...

PAUL: All of us! No excuses! Tonight! 7PM?

TRIXIE: Can I be your date?

PAUL: Just trying to figure out what corsage would go best with your lovely eyes. What's your favorite color?

TRIXIE: Expensive.

PAUL: Done. Now, I should let you and Max get on with it. Let me know if you need anything!

(Paul goes back into his office. Max comes out.)

MAX: Did you get our coffees, Trixie?

TRIXIE: Yes!

MAX: Where's...?

TRIXIE: ...I must have forgotten yours.

MAX: Oh. Well. Be a dear and run down and get me another one.

TRIXIE: I don't have any money.

(Max peels off another dollar bill from his roll.)

MAX: There should have been a lot of change...

TRIXIE: Back faster than you can dig a basement!

MAX: That's not... fast...

(Trixie exits.)

GWEN: She is a piece of work.

MAX: That she is. And unfortunately she works here. Well, these are the masonry designs. You are going to love it! Are you ready? One word. Gargoyles..

(He unfurls the blueprint to reveal a dour looking gargoyle with a man's face.)

GWEN: Dad?

MAX: I KNEW you'd love it!

GWEN: Gargoyles. On a retirement center. How much of this was your idea?

MAX: Oh, it was all mine. I'm about feel and aesthetic. Paul sees to the more mundane details. Load bearing walls and such.

GWEN: He gave me the impression it was the other way around.

MAX: Did he? It is so silly that we are here discussing Paul when we could be discussing much more pleasant topics…

GWEN: Like what?

MAX: Like what you are doing for dinner tonight?

GWEN: As a matter of fact, Paul invited me to join you at the Grove tonight. You and he and Trixie?

MAX: Splendid… just an intimate little gathering of you… and me… and Paul…

(Trixie comes in wearing a hat.)

TRIXIE: And me! *(Max takes the cup and turns it upside-down. It is empty.)* I got thirsty.

MAX: Is that a new hat?

(In unison, Trixie guiltily crosses to her desk and Gwen crosses to the door.)

GWEN: I should leave you to it. Here is the check. And we are in business! See you tonight? 7PM?

(As Gwen gets the check out of her purse, Max throws the empty cup and the masonry designs over his shoulder and Trixie catches them.)

MAX: Glorious!

GWEN: See you then!

(Gwen smiles warmly and exits.)

MAX: What a woman!

TRIXIE: If you're into those sorts of things.

MAX: What sorts of things?

(In gibberish, Trixie does an impersonation of Gwen's last line.)

MAX: And I am. We are on our way! Paul! PAUL! Get out here!

(Paul comes out of his office.)

PAUL: What's the news?

MAX: She paid us the money!

PAUL: That's jake!

MAX: It's enough to pay Ruby!

PAUL: Who's Ruby?

MAX: The woman who helped me borrow the money!

PAUL: Swell! We're in the clear?

MAX: Well... aside from the interest...

PAUL: How much?

MAX: Five for four.

PAUL: Five for four. Max. That's extortion!

MAX: We needed the money!

PAUL: Who did you borrow it from?

MAX: Deleoni & Sons.

PAUL: Oh no, Max. Oh no. You didn't.

MAX: What? We got the money. They gave us a cut rate on contractors. Things are looking up for the first time in months!

PAUL: Max...

MAX: What?

PAUL: Max. Do you know who the Deleoni family is?

MAX: Sure! They're a... family... a wealthy family... looking for investment opportunities.

PAUL: Max, they are the biggest crime family in the city and you just hired them to build the police commissioner's retirement home for police officers.

MAX: What?

PAUL: You just hired the people they put in jail to construct the retirement center for the people who put them in jail.

MAX: No.

PAUL: Yes.

MAX: Oh no.

PAUL: Oh yes.

MAX: This can't be right. There must be some misunderstanding. I met a very nice lady in the restaurant who happened to know someone who liked to make loans...

PAUL: You signed us up to work with the mob.

MAX: The mob?

PAUL: The mob.

TRIXIE: I thought Vito said we were going into waste management?

MAX: Dear god. We don't—! I... What are we going to do?

PAUL: Get fitted for cement shoes?

TRIXIE: Do they come in a flirty heel?

MAX: I signed nothing.

PAUL: Except for Gwen's contract with the city.

MAX: But not with Vito! We just shook on it! We'll just cancel the entire project and no one will be the wiser! We'll tell Vito the project was cancelled. There's no record we ever hired him, so it will be like it never even happened!

PAUL: Oh, Max... You think you can just... cancel... a contract... with the mob?

MAX: I can't breathe. I can't... I... *(Max goes into the kitchen to commit suicide)* The toaster cord isn't long enough to reach the sink...

PAUL: It's okay. Trixie didn't pay the water bill.

(Max runs out of the kitchen.)

MAX: PAUL! WHAT ARE WE GOING TO DO?

PAUL: Okay… okay… it can't be that bad—

MAX: It is! It is THAT bad!

PAUL: We should think this through.

MAX: Listen, Paul, if we don't finish this contract, we're going under. We are this close. THIS CLOSE! We can't fail! Not in front of Gwen Gladwell!

PAUL: We will figure something out.

MAX: I think I love her.

PAUL: You think you love everyone you ever meet.

TRIXIE: How come he never fell in love with me?

PAUL: He is intimidated by your intellect.

TRIXIE: I could play dumb.

MAX: NO! Listen. Gwen doesn't need to… know.

PAUL: What?

MAX: How would she ever find out who we hired to pound a nail or two… unless someone told her.

PAUL: Well, I'M not telling her.

MAX: And neither am I…

TRIXIE: Tell her what?

MAX: All we have to do is keep it together until we can pay back the loan in full. No one will be the wiser! I'll just… we'll simply expand the project by 20%. I'll ask Gwen tonight. She'll do it. For me.

PAUL: Max, don't use Gwen like that.

MAX: This is our last chance. It will be fine! The project will go forward! What could go wrong?

> *(Sirens and gunfire go off outside the window. Vito enters carrying a violin case.)*

VITO: Hey! I…uh… need to store my violin here for a little while. Okay? Oh! And if the coppers come up, you are an architectural firm. You got that? An arch-i-tec-tural firm.

> *(Vito goes into Max's office and slams the door as the chaos outside continues.)*

PAUL: What could go wrong?

(END OF ACT I)

Act II

Scene 1

Evening at the Grove. Max and Gwen enter and Max pulls out the chair for her at a table. Max is nervous and preoccupied.

GWEN: How many years has it been since we had dinner together, Max?

MAX: What a wonderful occasion to restart the clock! I… WE… are in your debt, Gwen.

GWEN: Oh, you.

MAX: I'm glad we have this opportunity to talk. Alone. Just you and I. About the project---

GWEN: Funny how it brought us back together.

MAX: I know! After all these years! And now we get to work together. So… what do you say we have a good chin waggle about work!

GWEN: It has been such a long time…

MAX: Some might say the years have flown by… but not me! Know I am so sincerely grateful that you hired us… especially after what went on between you and I…

GWEN: Ancient history.

MAX: Fantastic.

GWEN: You have no idea how much I wanted this chance to set things right.

MAX: Well, all is set to right as of right now. So---

GWEN: The way we parted has haunted me all these years. I have so many regrets…

MAX: Oh my...

GWEN: Did you have any idea how much you broke my heart?

MAX: No. I what? I mean--- I'm… sorry…?

GWEN: And then the way I broke things off...

MAX: I REALLY didn't notice. I MEAN! I… think… I… just… thought… if I was as… horrible… as possible, you would be able to move on more easily!

GWEN: Is that why?

MAX: Sure. OF COURSE! That's why! I did it for you. So you could be free! I was holding you back. I saw greatness in you! Which, strangely, leads me back to your father's project---

GWEN: I loved you so much. I never loved again.

MAX: Oh. I... um... well. You, too...

GWEN: So, I'm more than just a "friend of a friend"?

MAX: Whatever would have made you think...

GWEN: Oh, just a silly little conversation I had with Paul.

MAX: Oh. Paul. PAUL said that I said you were just a friend of a friend.

GWEN: It was a nothing comment. But you wanted to talk about the project.

MAX: Eh, we can get to that later... What else did he say? Was this when he asked you out for coffee?

GWEN: He is a good friend to you.

MAX: I suppose if you are into those sorts of things. You know, why are we even talking about him? Let's talk about us. You... and me... and not Paul...

(Trixie and Paul enter.)

PAUL: I appreciate you coming out with me, Trixie!

TRIXIE: That's what secretaries are for. Which I wish Max would figure out.

PAUL: Speak of the devil, there he is!

TRIXIE: With Gwen. I just don't get how she can come waltzing in here, taking my fiancé.

PAUL: Aw! She's a swell enough girl. Tell you what. Out of the goodness of my heart and because you've always been my favorite, I am going to break Max and Gwen up for you.

TRIXIE: You are!

PAUL: Just for you. Consider it my gift for the wedding Max doesn't know is happening.

TRIXIE: Go get 'em, tiger.

(Trixie and Paul sit down at the table.)

PAUL: Gwen! Max! Pleasure to see you both tonight. Shall we start with some caviar?

MAX: Oh, I don't know if that is necessary…

PAUL: Please! It is a celebration! Gwen? Order anything you like. It's on Max. He's loaded.

GWEN: Oh! The mussels look divine.

MAX: Of course.

TRIXIE: I would like the lobster.

MAX: No, you wouldn't.

TRIXIE: The steak.

MAX: No.

TRIXIE: Chicken?

MAX: Perhaps a round of crackers. For the table.

PAUL: Have you seen our waiter?

MAX: Service is terrible. Gwen? How about a spin around the dance floor?

GWEN: I would love that.

> *(Max and Gwen get up. Max leans over his shoulder to hiss at Paul.)*

MAX: If you would excuse us, Paul, I'm going to be taking my friend-of-a-friend for a foX. TroT. *(As Max leads Gwen onto the dance floor, Trixie storms off.)* You know, Gwen, I feel bad about the way things ended, too. You're right. Fate DID bring us together and after our conversation, I think I would like to see you more.

GWEN: I would like that very much.

MAX: I mean… not just as a client…

GWEN: That would be lovely.

MAX: Although, if you expanded the scope of the building, it would mean we would have to see each other every day. For years!

GWEN: That is an idea.

MAX: Think on it! We could build the foundation of our relationship into the foundation of this project. You! Me! And we would only need 20% more in advance to cover the additional costs.

GWEN: I'll… think on it.

MAX: Every day!

GWEN: It is a lot to take in. But… maybe…

MAX: Oh, Gwen! You never let me down. Tonight, we revel in the moon. The music! I'm a man! You're a woman! *(He looks over and sees Ruby enter.)* Oh god! *(Max shoves Gwen into a potted plant.)*

PAUL: Max?

MAX: Ruby is right. there. Distract Gwen.

(Max runs over to Ruby. Paul goes over to Gwen who is pulling herself out from the plant.)

PAUL: Sorry. Max is…indisposed. I'm afraid you shall have to put up with me for the time being.

(As Paul steers Gwen out onto the dance floor. Max grabs Ruby by the elbow and steers her to the other side of the stage.)

MAX: Fancy meeting you here!

RUBY: I like the way you rub my nickels together.

MAX: Funny you mention nickels. I have a whole stack of really good ones for you.

RUBY: Really…

MAX: Yes. You see. Our little boat has finally come in and we are able to pay you back almost in full.

RUBY: Almost in full?

MAX: In full! It is just the interest. So. We'll get that for you with the next job. But in the meantime, we won't be requiring your services any longer.

RUBY: Oh, doll. I think you have got it all wrong. Interest is all I've got in you.

MAX: I'm sorry. What?

RUBY: Oh, I have decided to take you on as my own personal pet to make sure you get lots of hands on attention.

(Ruby caresses Max and he is completely powerless against her charms.)

MAX: There will be no hands.

RUBY: Now, Max. Me and my boys are veerrry interested in this little police project and we are going to make sure that it stays strictly to schedule. We wouldn't want to have any problems during erection.

MAX: Construction.

RUBY: And I'm afraid that until you pay back that interest in full, you're mine.

MAX: Oh. Oh, this is bad...

RUBY: Only if we do it right.

MAX: I think... I think we can come up with some payment terms that are mutually beneficial.

RUBY: What'dya say we go up to my room to discuss delivery methods.

(Ruby and Max exit.)

GWEN: What is that about?

PAUL: Um… nothing.

GWEN: Oh.

PAUL: It's not you. You're lovely. It's him. He's… not.

GWEN: Oh. Well… it is very kind of you to keep me company…

PAUL: Anything for a client.

GWEN: You're a good friend.

PAUL: Well, he was the lead on our university curling team. I always swept for him.

GWEN: Still doing it I see.

PAUL: Old habits die hard… Splendid evening.

GWEN: Yes. Max was saying that right before he shoved me into a potted plant.

PAUL: It's a sign that he likes you.

GWEN: Is he with that other woman?

PAUL: Who, Max? No… he has a thing for plants is all. And wanted you to see that one up close.

GWEN: Paul.

PAUL: You're lovely. And she is… not. She is simply a former client and I'm sure he's just tying up loose ends.

(*They dance, lost in thought.*)

GWEN: Do you have someone in your life who could show up on your doorstep… and no matter what happened between you, you would just have to say yes? Do you have anyone like that in your life?

PAUL: I have no idea what you're talking about.

GWEN: I finally broke things off with Max all those years ago to keep myself safe… and wondered all this time if I was wrong… if I could have done something differently…

PAUL: Could you have?

GWEN: I don't know anymore. What if I was right?

PAUL: Do you think you were?

(*Max enters, disheveled.*)

GWEN: My head is spinning.

PAUL: It could be vertigo. From falling into a plant.

GWEN: It is all so complicated.

PAUL: I think that if things seem complicated, it's because you don't like the answer.

GWEN: If only life were as simple as building a building. You start with a foundation and put up some walls and a roof, and pretty soon you have a home.

PAUL: You forgot that every building has stress put on the joists and sometimes the materials are not strong enough to hold.

GWEN: But your designs don't have those problems... The lines are straightforward. And bold.

PAUL: Well, straightforward is what I do best.

GWEN: Nothing to distract from the imperfections. Just high quality construction.

PAUL: Yes.

GWEN: They say you can tell a lot about an architect by his buildings.

PAUL: Unfortunately, Max doesn't design anything except gargoyles.

GWEN: But you do.

PAUL: Yes, I do.

GWEN: Yes, you do.

PAUL: Oh.

GWEN: Oh.

(They stop, lost in each other's eyes.)

PAUL: Maybe we should get back to Max.

GWEN: Right.

(They walk back over to the table.)

MAX: You're back! Why don't you sit down! Or better yet, call it an evening.

GWEN: We just got here.

MAX: And I am bushed.

PAUL: I think what Max is trying to say is that he and his former client have a little bit of business to attend to… in private.

GWEN: Oh. In private. In practically the middle of the night. How interesting.

MAX: How dare you! You are my… Gwen. And she? She… is… business.

(Trixie enters.)

PAUL: He is just closing her contract.

TRIXIE: Before she opens a new contract on us.

GWEN: What?

PAUL: This is supposed to be a celebration of the new project! And your reunion after so many years with Max. Max Max Max… And Gwen. So perfect. The two of you. So, Gwen, what do you say I meet you in the bar while Max sees to his... Ruby. His client, Ruby. Who is NOTHING to him compared to you.

GWEN: (*pointedly*) That would be lovely.

> (*Gwen leaves the room with a look towards Paul. Max turns and points his finger at Paul.*)

MAX: Et tu, Brute?

PAUL: What?

MAX: I'm gone for five minutes?

PAUL: What?

MAX: I don't like the way Gwen was looking at you.

PAUL: I'm sorry?

MAX: And they way you were looking at Gwen!

PAUL: Yes. We made eye contact.

MAX: No. You were… looking… at her.

PAUL: What about that thing with you and Ruby?

MAX: THAT? That was me just trying to save our company! But you. OH! YOU!

PAUL: Saving the company?! You shoved a client into a potted plant!

MAX: Don't change the subject!

PAUL: Gwen and I danced. We looked at one another. It happens.

MAX: Oh, I have given that look. I KNOW that look.

PAUL: First off, I will look at whomever I like however I like, be it Gwen or anyone else. Second off, Gwen Gladwell is a grown woman and perfectly capable of deciding who she wants to look at her and who she would not. IF I was looking at her, which I was not.

TRIXIE: Please don't fight.

MAX: I saw you! Mooning over here like some sick schoolboy!

PAUL: And what, exactly, did that alleged look "look" like so I can make sure never to do it again?

MAX: Oh? Like this.

(Max strolls across the room and gives Paul an exaggerated look, batting his eyes.)

PAUL: If I gave her that look, I would have been tossed onto the street for indecent behavior.

MAX: Well, it looks different if I'm... just... doing it. But I saw it! Between the two of you!

PAUL: Aw, nuts!

TRIXIE: Please don't fight.

(Max grabs Trixie and stands her up, using her in place of Gwen, demonstrating what he saw go on between Gwen and Paul.)

MAX: You looked at her like this. And then you did this. And I saw you do THIS!

(Paul spins Trixie around to demonstrate his side of the story.)

PAUL: I think what you saw was me looking at her like this. And then I did this. And then I did this and brought her back to you.

TRIXIE: Please don't fight.

(Max spins Trixie around and demonstrates.)

MAX: You most DEFINITELY did this.

(Paul spins Trixie around and demonstrates.)

PAUL: It was only this.

(Max spins Trixie around and demonstrates.)

MAX: Oh, you might have been doing that, but you were most definitely leading up to this.

(He gives Trixie a kiss. Paul yanks Trixie out of his arms.)

PAUL: Oh, if I was going to do that, I wouldn't do it like that. I'd do it like THIS!

(He gives Trixie a passionate kiss.)

TRIXIE: Please fight.

MAX: I may have flirted with Ruby and done what is necessary for the health of this company, but if I find out that you touched so much as a hair on Gwen's head, I swear to the heavens above, Paul, and all the wickedness below…

PAUL: What?

MAX: Just. Don't.

(Max exits.)

TRIXIE: What don't you want him to do? You could show me.

(END OF SCENE)

Act II

Scene 2

Morning the next day. Office. Max enters in last night's tux. It has been a rough night. His hair is messed. There are bags under his eyes. Trixie is highly caffeinated.

TRIXIE: Morning, boss!

MAX: Don't speak.

TRIXIE: Whew! Was that a night last night or what I brewed a whole pot of coffee to get us through the day. But there's something very important I have to tell you I received a call and I think it is a call that you are going to be very interested in and I wrote down the message somewhere on a piece of paper and then carefully set it aside but I can't remember oh where did I put that message it is so unlike me to lose a message I know that I put it in here somewhere but as soon as I find it I think it is something you are going to want to address—

> *(Max crosses, not paying any attention to Trixie, goes into his office, and slams the door. NOTE: Trixie's*

line is a ramble and can be cut at any point to sync with staging. Paul comes in the front door.)

PAUL: Morning, Trixie!

TRIXIE: Morning, Paul!

PAUL: Heard from Gwen?

TRIXIE: She just phoned. Said the mayor can hardly wait to find out what we're up to!

PAUL: Let us know the moment she gets in. Have you told Max?

(Max comes out of his office and sees Paul.)

MAX: Trixie? Would you tell Paul that I have a meeting with the Deleoni contractors this morning?

TRIXIE: Paul? Max has a meeting with the Deleoni contractors this morning.

PAUL: Trixie? Would you ask him if he has enough money to pay them off?

TRIXIE: Max? Do you have enough money to pay them off?

MAX: Tell Paul that the finances are my affair.

TRIXIE: He's having an affair.

MAX: I am not having an affair!

TRIXIE: He's not having an affair. But he has not said whether or not he has any money which he may or may not have been using for his "not an affair."

PAUL: Really, Max.

> *(Max goes to pour himself a cup of coffee. Trixie clears her throat. Max takes a handful of coins out of his pocket and throws them across the stage in the general direction of the coffee kitty.)*

MAX: I will kindly ask you to keep your nose out of my business. I have the contractors this morning.

PAUL: And a photo-op with Gwen and the mayor.

MAX: Oh no…

> *(Max downs cup after cup, finally resorting to drinking the coffee straight out of the carafe.)*

PAUL: Oh, yes! Looking fresh as a daisy, Max. Say, what'd you and Ruby get up to last night? Did you manage to sever our ties with the mob before this very public meeting with the most powerful politicians in our city?

MAX: Not exactly…

PAUL: Not exactly?

MAX: I paid her some interest… with the promise that we will pay her later in full. Believe you me, I am sacrificing for this company.

PAUL: I'll make sure Trixie notes your overtime hours.

TRIXIE: Does that mean I pay him double or half?

PAUL: I think last night was pro bono.

MAX: I smoothed things over… from one professional to another…

PAUL: Oh, she is a professional all right.

MAX: And all they ask is that we be available whenever the Deleoni family needs a hand with some work…

PAUL: Just how shoddy was your handiwork last night?

MAX: Don't.

PAUL: You should have stayed with us if that was the best you could do.

MAX: Why? So I could watch you steal Gwen Gladwell away from me?

PAUL: How can you even be angry at me about Gwen when you're off building a skyscraper of love with the head of the Deleoni family?

MAX: Don't you even! I love Gwen!

PAUL: Since when?

MAX: Since she told me I broke her heart!

PAUL: That woman deserves more than your pity.

MAX: You tried to chase Gwen away with that "friend-of-a-friend" business!

PAUL: Those were your exact words!

MAX: You're only interested in her because you're seething with jealousy!

PAUL: Who's seething?!

MAX: You are!

PAUL: Nothing happened between me and Gwen!

MAX: Sure! I'm sure you stayed up all night playing Old Maid.

PAUL: Our interactions were perfectly appropriate.

TRIXIE: I was there!

MAX: Trixie wouldn't know inappropriate behavior if it came along and goosed her from behind.

TRIXIE: Knowing inappropriate behavior and enjoying inappropriate behavior are two entirely different things.

MAX: You couldn't wait to pour your cement on top of our gently curing form!

PAUL: It cured years ago.

MAX: You ruined our mixture before we could even set.

PAUL: You're the one adding EXCESS FLUIDS!

MAX: You pounced upon the cracks in our foundation AND BENT THE REBAR OF OUR LOVE!

PAUL: YOUR SUBBASE IS UNSTABLE!

MAX: BECAUSE THE INTEGRITY OF OUR SUBGRADE IS BEING SLUICED AWAY BY YOU!

PAUL: Gwen will be in later. You can talk to her yourself.

MAX: I will.

PAUL: Fine.

MAX: FINE!

(They both go into their offices and slam their doors simultaneously.)

TRIXIE: Anyone want coffee?

(Vito enters carrying a briefcase.)

VITO: TRIXIE!

TRIXIE: VITO!

VITO: How's my girl?

TRIXIE: I still got it!

VITO: I'll say you do.

TRIXIE: Say I'll do what?

VITO: What?

TRIXIE: What do you say I do?

VITO: It.

TRIXIE: I do it?

VITO: No, you got it!

TRIXIE: Got what?

VITO: It.

TRIXIE: It?

VITO: It!

TRIXIE: It? Oh. OH! I got it!

VITO & TRIXIE: AY!

> *(Max and Paul come out of their offices. They both see Vito. Paul glares at Max and goes back inside.)*

MAX: VITO! So glad you could come in today.

VITO: Like I always say, when you work with guys like me, you're working with professionals.

MAX: Professionals indeed. I have some paperwork I need you to look over. Could you join me in my office?

VITO: Sure thing!

> *(Max and Vito go into Max's office and slam the door. Gwen enters.)*

TRIXIE: *(shouting)* She's here!

GWEN: Morning, Trixie!

TRIXIE: Morning! Want a cup of coffee?

GWEN: Sure! Let me get you a nickel.

TRIXIE: Don't worry about it! We'll just charge it to Max's paycheck. His treat!

GWEN: I'm not sure—

TRIXIE: You're a client! And the Marshalls pride themselves on treating their clients well.

> *(Trixie pours herself a cup of coffee and walks past Gwen.)*

GWEN: All right then. Is Paul in?

TRIXIE: Sure is! PAUL!

> *(Paul opens his door.)*

PAUL: GWEN! So good to see you! It is a good day here at TF Architecture.

> *(He leaps over to her and hustles her towards his office.)*

GWEN: My!

PAUL: Have we got the team together for you! YES!

GWEN: Yes, what?

PAUL: Yes, you have arrived!

GWEN: Yes, I have. Listen, I feel bad about the way I left things last night with Max. Could I...? Trixie, is Max here?

TRIXIE: Sure is! Right—

PAUL: —after he gets back.

GWEN: What?

PAUL: He isn't here now, but he will be. Right after he gets back.

TRIXIE: But I just saw him—

PAUL: —go into a meeting. But he wants me to go over some of the details of the retirement center with you. Will you?

GWEN: I suppose.

PAUL: Trixie will let us know the moment Max gets back. I promise!

> *(Paul and Gwen disappear into Paul's office and slam the door. Max comes out.)*

MAX: Trixie, could you grab some coffee for Vito and me?

TRIXIE: PAUL! *(The door opens and Paul's head pops out.)* Max is here.

PAUL/MAX: No, he's/I'm not.

TRIXIE: Yes he is. *(Max hides.)* Oh, I guess he's not.

GWEN: Did I hear Max's voice?

(*Gwen comes out.*)

TRIXIE/PAUL: Yes./No.

PAUL: Apologies for the interruption. I'll be just a moment. (*Gwen goes back in*) Trixie! I need you to hide Max from Gwen.

TRIXIE: For how long?

PAUL: How long would you like?

TRIXIE: Forty years.

PAUL: Perfect.

(*Paul goes back into the office. Max pops back up.*)

TRIXIE: Oh, there you are! Just where I left you.

(*Vito comes out.*)

VITO: What about that coffee? Hey, Trixie! What do you say I take you out sometime for a milkshake.

TRIXIE: I don't drink milkshakes on a first date.

MAX: This is all splendid. Why don't you take her out now—

(*The door to Paul's office opens and Gwen comes out.*)

GWEN: Maybe Trixie can ring him—

(Max pushes Trixie into Vito and they fall down together behind the desk.)

MAX: Ah! You're here!

GWEN: Yes. I wanted to speak with you...

MAX: Well, wait no longer! Let's go!

GWEN: I left my purse in Paul's office.

MAX: Well in you go!

(He shoves Gwen into Paul's office. Vito and Trixie get up from behind the desk.)

VITO: So, how many dates before you usually do that?

TRIXIE: We might be engaged

(Max comes out as the door opens and Ruby walks in. Vito sees Ruby and pushes Trixie down in a panic.)

MAX: Ruby! What a pleasure! What can I do for you today?

RUBY: I think the better question is what can you do to me today?

MAX: Let me take you out—

RUBY: Some money of mine went missing, Max.

MAX: Oh?

RUBY: And now I need a quiet little company—

MAX: —the neighbors are a nightmare—

RUBY: —with a large cash flow—

MAX: —we're not that large—

RUBY: —and messy accounting.

MAX: Trixie is tops with the paperwork!

RUBY: And it made me think of you.

MAX: Thanks?

RUBY: It's a hard situation but I think you're up to it.

MAX: Oh.

RUBY: This shouldn't take any longer than fifteen minutes.

(Max and Ruby go into Max's office. Vito and Trixie rise.)

VITO: You gotta hide me!

TRIXIE: Oh? Are we playing sardines? I'll close my eyes and count to 100.

VITO: Listen, Trixie. You my girl?

TRIXIE: I'm letting you take me out for a milkshake.

VITO: I got two thousand smackers for Ruby.

TRIXIE: Well, just kiss her already!

VITO: No! Cashola! Listen. I got that missing money. I was supposed to get it laundered but I ran outta time.

TRIXIE: Oh, you just leave that to me. I'm smooth with laundering.

VITO: Really?

TRIXIE: Sure! I do it all the time for Max.

VITO: Never would have taken that chump for the numbers racket.

TRIXIE: Oh, he doesn't play tennis.

VITO: What?

TRIXIE: What?

(Vito gives her his briefcase.)

VITO: Okay, take this. You didn't see me. Trixie, you're a treasure!

> *(Trixie heads for the kitchen. Vito crawls out the door just as Gwen and Paul step out of Paul's office.)*

GWEN: The mayor won't wait. Where did he go?

PAUL: Wait!

> *(She opens up the door to Max's office and then closes it. Max comes out of the room disheveled.)*

MAX: This is not what it looks like!

GWEN: How dare you!

MAX: This is just business!

GWEN: I was a fool!

MAX: She is just our loan officer!

GWEN: Well enjoy your full service banking!

> *(Gwen runs out.)*

MAX: GWEN!

PAUL: Now you've done it… Gwen!

> *(Paul runs after her. Ruby steps into the doorway of Max's office.)*

RUBY: Was that the police commissioner's daughter?

MAX: Yes. Yes, that's her.

RUBY: You know what, Max? I think I like being intimately involved with your work. In fact, I think it might be best if I installed a branch of operations right here. Partner.

MAX: Help!

> *(Ruby pulls Max into the room and shuts the door behind them. Trixie comes out of the kitchen with the soap and a bucket. She proceeds to wash Vito's money. Paul reenters, defeated.)*

PAUL: What are you doing?

TRIXIE: Laundering Vito's money.

PAUL: Oh. Don't forget the starch.

(END OF SCENE)

Act II

Scene 3

Morning. Max storms in the front door of the empty office.

MAX: Paul? Are you here? I am not speaking to you! PAUL!

    (Vito comes out of Max's office.)

VITO: Listen, Squinky just got picked up by the coppers. I'm running down there to post bail. Tell Ruby it was all a big misunderstanding. Or don't tell her anything at all! We'll get him on the TF payroll and everything will be right as rain.

MAX: I'm sorry. What—?

VITO: You're late.

MAX: My apologies…? TRIXIE! *(Trixie comes out of the kitchen.)* Um… yes… would you like a cup of coffee?

VITO: You buying?

MAX: Sure… Trixie? Coffee?

TRIXIE: You got a nickel?

MAX: Take it out of my paycheck.

TRIXIE: I already do.

MAX: What? (*Paul enters.*) You're late.

PAUL: My apologies. Was there a meeting I was not aware of?

VITO: Listen. Ruby's making some administrative changes here, just until this project is done.

MAX: Oh?

VITO: Don't you worry. You two got nothing to do but sit back and relax until we are all done with you. Oh! And stay out of my office!

(*Vito points at Max's office as he leaves.*)

MAX: OH! That is not right. That is not right at all. I did not sign up for this.

PAUL: Actually, you did. You literally signed us up for this. In a legally binding contract. With a seal from the

mayor's office. Which is on file for the whole world to see. I could get us copies in triplicate.

MAX: Rub it in! He said when we shook hands that we would settle any issues like gentlemen.

PAUL: Gentlemen usually solve their issues with pistols at dawn.

MAX: Wait. Is that what he meant?!

(Vito enters carrying a large roulette wheel.)

VITO: Trixie!

TRIXIE: Vito!

PAUL: Vito...? What's that?

VITO: Just ran into Larry the Fist. He thought those comatose retirees might need a little entertainment down in the basement. Gratis from the Deleoni family to yous.

TRIXIE: You're so thoughtful!

VITO: I'm always thinkin', doll!

TRIXIE: Next door to the speakeasy?

MAX: We do not have the construction funds for a... speakeasy.

VITO: Don't you worry. We're donating it to the cause.

PAUL: I can't let you do this.

VITO: I believe you can.

MAX: It is just soooo outside the scope of the project.

VITO: Consider it scoped. Ruby has already loaned you the money.

MAX: NO! No. I don't want any more loans or any more money…

VITO: Aw. Sure you do! Who doesn't love money?

(He goes into Max's office.)

PAUL: Speakeasy? The most important thing in Gwen's life is her father's reputation and you are letting the mob build a speakeasy in her project?

MAX: She doesn't have to know. We won't fill out the permits and then we won't be able to build it.

TRIXIE: Oh. They already filled out the forms.

MAX: Trixie? My darling?

TRIXIE: Yes, dear?

MAX: You have never done a day of work in your life. Please. PLEASE! Tell me you didn't file that paperwork.

TRIXIE: Of course I did! I decided that charmer in the permits office needed to ask me out on a second date.

MAX: She filed the permits. SHE FILED THE PERMITS! I need a fork and a light socket!

PAUL: You'd only blow the fuse and we'd have to borrow the money to buy a new one.

(*Vito comes out.*)

VITO: Hey! Could I get more ice, toots?

TRIXIE: Sure thing, sugar!

VITO: No, just ice.

(*Vito goes back in.*)

MAX: I don't like you talking to him.

TRIXIE: Aw, Max! Are you jealous?

MAX: No! No. The absolute last thing I am in this moment is jealous!

(*Vito comes out of the office.*)

VITO: Hey! Where's that ice?

TRIXIE: Max keeps interrupting me.

VITO: Max. Let the little lady do her job.

MAX: Why break a trend?

VITO: Did you make table arrangements for me and my family, toots?

TRIXIE: No. I just made reservations for dinner. But I can get you centerpieces if you want.

VITO: What?

TRIXIE: What?

VITO: You trying to be funny?

TRIXIE: Of course not! If I wanted to be funny, I'd say something like, "What do you get when you cross an amphibian with a Slavic nation?"… "A toad-pole".

(Max genuinely likes her joke.)

VITO: That's not funny.

TRIXIE: That's why I wasn't trying.

VITO: Ay! That's my girl.

TRIXIE: Don't let Max hear you. He gets very jealous.

VITO: Wait. You're sayin' she's YOUR dame? This here is MY dame.

MAX: Consider her a gift from me to you.

TRIXIE: Don't let him fool you. Why, the last time I so much as looked at another man, he burst into a fit of rage!

MAX: We missed a deadline because she took the fellow from the permits office out to lunch.

TRIXIE: See? Still seething with jealousy.

VITO: What sort of a gentleman are you? This here is a defenseless flower. She should be treated with tender, loving care.

(Vito kisses Trixie's hand.)

TRIXIE: Oh… Vito… A defenseless flower… Are you listening, Max?

MAX: As defenseless as an oleander.

VITO: Trixie, don't you listen to this bum. You come to me. I'll make sure you're treated right.

TRIXIE: You hear that, Max?

MAX: Now see here, Vito. Trixie is a good girl.

VITO: You telling me I don't know how to behave like a gentleman?

MAX: No! Not at all. You are a complete gentleman. But, Vito. VITO. I just feel this might not be working. Not you! Us! Rather than forcing your men to work harder... or at all... we were thinking it might be a better option to move on and pretend like this never even happened...

VITO: You want to pretend like this never even happened? You? Want to pretend? Like this never... HAPPENED!

MAX: I'm sorry! I'm sorry!

VITO: We don't like people who break their contracts. We tend to like to break other things in return.

MAX: Where did you get the idea I wanted out of our contract? Things are snazzy! Wonderful! We couldn't be happier!

VITO: That's what I like to hear. Good. Good. I would hate to have to replace you.

MAX: Replace...? Me....?

VITO: If it wasn't for you being a special friend of Trixie here...

(Max and Trixie lock eyes.)

MAX: Trixie?

VITO: A gentleman keeps his promises. And I would hate to have to upset her. *(Vito looks at Trixie and she gives him an accepting nod.)* Now, you just sit back and relax and this'll run like eggs in coffee. Trixie! Ice!

>   *(Vito goes into Max's office as Trixie scampers into the kitchen.)*

PAUL: We've got crooks on our payroll and illegal gambling dens in the basement of Gwen's dream project. You have got to put an end to this, Max!

MAX: Fine. I'll just... I'll just... How sharp is our paper cutter?

>   *(Max goes into Paul's office.)*

PAUL: It would barely make it through your vertebrae. Although, right now, I think you should give it a try! *(Gwen enters)* Gwen! You're here!

GWEN: I wanted to bring you a copy of the paper! The project made the front page!

PAUL: That is fabulous!

GWEN: I think it really turned out well. Did you find a contractor?

PAUL: Ah... Max did.

GWEN: Lovely! Oh. Do you think we should have included them in the picture with the mayor?

PAUL: No. Noooo... I think that would be a bad idea.

(Vito pops his head out.)

VITO: Why, hello!

GWEN: Hello.

VITO: Who's the dame?

PAUL: She's with me.

VITO: Lucky dog. Some real nice stems on that tomato. Hey, Trixie! Ice!

(Trixie runs from the kitchen into Max's office holding a pile of ice.)

GWEN: Do you know who that is?

PAUL: Yes.

GWEN: No. Do you KNOW who that IS??

PAUL: Aaaaaa business... associate...?

GWEN: PAUL! Why is Vito Deleoni in Max's office?

PAUL: So. You know Vito.

GWEN: Yes. Yes. My father is the commissioner of the police force. I know who Vito DELEONI is.

PAUL: Well... it is a funny thing. You see, Max accidentally hired the Deleoni family... to... build your project... Hardee-har-har-har?

GWEN: I'm not laughing.

PAUL: We were having some cash flow problems... and he...

GWEN: Stop sweeping things away for him, Paul.

PAUL: Max is an idiot and he borrowed money from the mob. We've been trying to pay them back, but they've taken a personal interest in your project.

GWEN: Oh, no!

PAUL: We'll figure a way out!

GWEN: I did it again! I trusted Max! And he destroyed everything! Like he always did! Why did I trust him?

PAUL: You didn't trust Max. You just hired him.

GWEN: I TRUSTED HIM! Oh... my father... his reputation... oh no... oh no oh no oh no...

(Paul gathers her up into his arms in comfort, quieting her down.)

PAUL: Shh! Shh! Shh! We will figure this out.

GWEN: You can't tell anyone.

PAUL: I won't.

GWEN: If this gets out…

PAUL: It won't…

GWEN: Oh Paul… The project is on the front page! With the mayor!

PAUL: Trust me. I'll get it sorted out. Even if it kills us.

GWEN: What if they kill us?

PAUL: That might be a best case scenario.

GWEN: What do we do?

PAUL: You leave it to me. I won't let you down.

GWEN: You never would, would you…

PAUL: I try…

GWEN: Thank you.

PAUL: Anything for… a client.

(Max comes storming through the office looking at his watch.)

PAUL: Max! A word.

MAX: Not now, Paul.

GWEN: NOW, Max.

MAX: I… of course. What can I do for you? Ready to expand the project scope?

GWEN: How can you even stand there and say that to me?

MAX: Oh no…

GWEN: Oh yes.

MAX: Oh NO!

PAUL: Oh—

MAX: You found out.

PAUL: She knows.

MAX: So. You know.

GWEN: What do you have to say for yourself?

MAX: Well, what do you expect me to do? If you hadn't been so cheap and given us such a small budget, we could have hired someone better!

GWEN: Cheap?

MAX: I told you. Just a 20% increase in scope and we would have been in the clear!

GWEN: It is like you don't even understand why this is important. It is like all you care about is you money and your scope. What did I ever see in you?

MAX: I have no idea! This was just supposed to be a job!

GWEN: It was never just a job. But it was to you. Wasn't it? Just a job.

PAUL: MAX! Stop! Ideas! Solutions!

MAX: I DON'T KNOW!

GWEN: Fine. FINE! Max isn't going to get us out of this...

MAX: ...it was all under control...

GWEN: ...so I guess I'll just have to save us all myself.

PAUL: Not by yourself.

MAX: SLUICER!

(Trixie comes out of the office with a steno pad and begins measuring the size of the floor by pacing it out.)

TRIXIE: One… two… three..

PAUL: Trixie? What are you doing?

TRIXIE: Just trying to figure out where we should put all the new office furniture…

MAX: No one asked you to order any office furniture.

TRIXIE: Well, where is everyone going to sit?

MAX: Where is who going to sit?

TRIXIE: All of the new employees starting Monday.

MAX: New employees?

TRIXIE: Vito said that six of his best guys will be here Monday to oversee our operation.

MAX: Dear god.

TRIXIE: Isn't it nice to have such hands-on management?

GWEN: Paul, we have to end this and we have to end this now. If you and Max and Trixie see the faces of those hatchet men, the Deleoni family will kill you before they let you free.

TRIXIE: So should I cancel this bulk order of dumpsters?

GWEN: Only if they're too small to hide a body in.

TRIXIE: (*consults her steno pad*) You should be able to fit at least ten or fifteen in there. Twenty if you stack them end-to-end and really pack them in.

GWEN: I'm fairly certain they'll only need room for four.

TRIXIE: That'll work..

> (*Max raises a ball peen hammer from Trixie's desk to kill himself. Vito comes out of the office with his hat and violin case.*)

VITO: Hey Trixie! Grab your things!

TRIXIE: What's up?

VITO: You're with me!

TRIXIE: But Max...

VITO: Trust me, toots. As long as you're with me, Max and Paul will be just fine.

MAX: No, I need her here—

VITO: She's with ME. And like I said, as long as she is with me, you gentlemen. are. FINE.

(*They leave.*)

MAX: I don't like the way he was looking at her.

GWEN: You care?

MAX: Of course I care! It's Trixie!

GWEN: Oh. Oh. Trixie. I can't believe I was so blind.

PAUL: What?

GWEN: It's always been Trixie.

MAX: What?

GWEN: TRIXIE!

MAX: We're not doing anything which puts her in danger…

PAUL: She's already in danger. What's your idea?

GWEN: She's got Vito wrapped around her little finger. With a few more fingers, that woman could bring Vito to his knees.

MAX: Trixie? Our dear, sweet, utterly clueless Trixie? When Hoover became president, she thought we elected a vacuum.

GWEN: She's brought you to your knees on more than one occasion.

MAX: We're not talking about me! I just don't know if she…

GWEN: Oh, know that she is. You've never seen what she is, have you Max? Have you? But you have, Paul.

PAUL: She's always been the ace in our sleeve.

GWEN: Think, Max! Think! Who is the one person who drives you batty? Who pushes you to the brink every day? Who is so backwards, she managed to hoodwink you two into naming this firm after her? We sic Trixie on them and help her do what she does and the mob won't see what hit 'em.

PAUL: Oh, Gwen! I could kiss you!

GWEN: Okay.

MAX: What?

GWEN: Never mind. Trust me, Max. You want to go toe-to-toe with the mob? Trixie is your man.

MAX: This is foolish—

GWEN: Can I count on you, Paul?

PAUL: Always.

MAX: This is the worst idea—

PAUL: MAX!

MAX: It IS!

GWEN: Worse than hiring the mob? Worse than lying about it? Worse than using people for your own selfish purposes and putting their lives at risk because of your deception?

MAX: ...maybe?

GWEN: Trust me. Trust her. Tomorrow we unleash Operation Trixie.

(END OF SCENE)

Act II

Scene 4

The next morning. Office. Max, Paul, Gwen are looking at the door intently. Gwen directs all of the action in the scene. Trixie enters.

GWEN & PAUL: TRIXIE!

TRIXIE: SURPRISE! No, wait. That's what you're supposed to say... Should there be party hats?

PAUL: Trixie, let me get your hat.

GWEN: Trixie, have some coffee.

> *(Gwen hands her a cup of coffee.)*

PAUL: Trixie, sit right down here.

> *(Paul sits her down into a wheeled chair and pushes her towards her desk.)*

GWEN: Comfortable?

PAUL: Need more coffee?

GWEN & PAUL: TRIXIE!

TRIXIE: You are getting me all spun around.

(Paul and Gwen start spinning her in her chair.)

GWEN: Spun around you say?

PAUL: Like this?

GWEN: Or like this?

TRIXIE: STOP! *(They stop.)* Okay, let's go again!
WHEEEEE!

(They push Trixie behind her desk.)

GWEN: Trixie, we need your help desperately… there
is a very important deadline and we absolutely must
have the permit filed before noon.

PAUL: Form B must be delivered to City Hall.

GWEN: Yes. Form B.

TRIXIE: You're letting me do the paperwork again?

MAX: I have been told you're the only one capable of
steering our boat into this iceberg.

TRIXIE: Flatterer.

MAX: Do you seriously think she can keep this straight?

> *(Gwen directs Max and Paul to begin piling the paperwork in front of Trixie. NOTE: All numbers should be spoken individually, i.e. 1675 should be read "one-six-seven-five" instead of "sixteen-seventy-five.")*

PAUL: Of course! So Form B must be delivered to City Hall, but only after Form 137 has been registered with the land lease. And prior to that, there is Form 1675. As well as form 852.

GWEN: Oh! And don't forget form 467.

PAUL: Ah, yes! Form 467. That is a tough one. It will require form 389, form 236, and form 371b.

GWEN: Oh dear… Trixie? Would you be a dear and explain this all to Vito for us? We're in the midst of a very time sensitive project.

PAUL: And we know that you…

GWEN: …our dear Trixie…

PAUL: …would handle it best. Think you got it?

TRIXIE: So… register form 137 and then form B at City hall, but prior to that, ensure that form 467, form 389, form 236, and form 317b have been handled?

MAX: How—

PAUL: Always told you, Max. She's a treasure!

(*Vito walks in.*)

VITO: Trixie!

TRIXIE: Vito!

VITO: Fellas.

MAX & PAUL: Vito.

VITO: Dame.

(*Gwen gives him a sarcastic curtsy.*)

TRIXIE: Vito, I can't talk right now. I have a very important deadline.

VITO: Aw, toots. When you're working with the Deleoni family, there are no such thing as deadlines.

TRIXIE: Oh! But if I don't file form 371b, it is going to cost you $300.

VITO: What's $300 between friends?

TRIXIE: Well, it compounds with interest if I don't get it filed prior to form 236.

VITO: Okay, so file form 236 and let me get you some champagne from my private stock.

TRIXIE: Would you sign this, please?

VITO: Sure.

TRIXIE: And this.

VITO: Right.

TRIXIE: And this.

VITO: Okay.

TRIXIE: And this and this and this.

VITO: Hey! Hey! Hey! You're giving me hand cramps. What's all this autograph hounding?

> (*Without pausing to take a breath, Trixie places paper after paper in front of Vito and rattles off the information.*)

TRIXIE: If we don't file form 371b prior to form 236, we'll get stuck doing an addendum 536.12. But that is nothing if we don't get them all in before form 389. Because it will hold up form 467, which means that our land lease will fall through and we'll have to file form1675 in triplicate with the State, but only if we get it done before form 852. Because they all have to be delivered to City Hall if we hope to file Form B.

VITO: That's a lot of papers.

TRIXIE: So sign 371b.

VITO: Done.

PAUL: Wait! He signed 317b, not 371b.

TRIXIE: Form 236 will fix it.

GWEN: I have it here!

VITO: Okay.

TRIXIE: But was form 236 before 371b?

PAUL: Oo! He'll need to sign the addendum.

> (*Max holds up the addendum and Paul grabs it and brings it over.*)

TRIXIE: You're right! Now we have to do form 852 because you signed form 236 after form 371b.

VITO: I was just doing what you told me!

GWEN: Did you get form 1675?

VITO: Didn't we sign that one already?

TRIXIE: That was form 852. This is 1675. It has to be done before form 467.

VITO: Who needs to file all this paperwork? Them cops are so dumb, they won't even notice.

TRIXIE: Perhaps we should dictate it for you so you don't get confused.

> (*She motions to the Dictaphone. Gwen snaps her fingers and Paul rolls it over.*)

MAX: Trixie, did you get the Dictaphone repaired?

VITO: What's a Dictaphone?

PAUL: It seems stuck.

> (*Trixie bangs on the machine with a ball peen hammer.*)

TRIXIE: (*to the Dictaphone*) Hello, Dictaphone? (*to Vito as she tosses the hammer away*) I'll need you to dictate a letter.

VITO: Why would I dictate a letter?

TRIXIE: Because I need to see if the machine works, and if you don't, I won't know what to type.

VITO: You don't need to type anything right now.

TRIXIE: Need and want are two entirely different things.

VITO: So what you're saying is you want to type a letter?

TRIXIE: I want what you want. Isn't that what you want? Me to want your wants?

VITO: Well, yes…

TRIXIE: So if I want to type a letter, and I want what you want, it must mean that you want me to type it, because otherwise I wouldn't want to.

VITO: You're makin' me dizzy.

TRIXIE: Oh, my darling Vito, it's simple! You just sit right down here and say into the Dictaphone exactly what you want me to type.

> (*She sits at the ready.*)

VITO: I don't know what I want you to type.

TRIXIE: Well, while you think, sign form 469.

> (*She passes Vito the form to sign and then begins typing.*)

VITO: 469?

TRIXIE: 469. And we'll need your boss's signature.

VITO: Boss?

TRIXIE: Who's your boss?

VITO: My boss is Ruby Deleoni.

TRIXIE: Is she your big boss?

VITO: She's the biggest boss there is.

TRIXIE: I'll just need to type her name into this form.

(*Vito sits down*)

VITO: I don't want you typing her name anywhere.

TRIXIE: But the form...

VITO: That woman runs the biggest gaming operations in town and I don't want no one or nothing to have her name typed down on any form whatever that's going to City Hall.

(*Gwen and Paul exchange a triumphant glance.*)

TRIXIE: Okay, but we'll have to fill out from 6qr5.

VITO: So fill out form 6qr5.

TRIXIE: Now, Vito... my sweet Vito... I'm only doing my job.

VITO: It is a lot for just walking through the door.

GWEN: Let me get you a cup of coffee. Oh, is this yours?

(Picks up Vito's briefcase.)

VITO: Hey! Hey! Put that down!

(Gwen drops it.)

TRIXIE: It's okay! The money isn't in it.

GWEN: Oh! Was there money in it?

VITO: Merely some administrative fees.

MAX: What administrative fees?!

(Paul speaks directly into the Dictaphone receiver.)

PAUL: First I heard of it! Did Ruby know about these administrative fees?

VITO: Don't none of you worry about the money which is no longer in that briefcase.

PAUL: We really should let her know it is missing.

VITO: She don't need to know what she don't know.

(Trixie takes the receiver from Paul and speaks directly into it.)

TRIXIE: Vito was just tidying it up for her. He laundered it.

VITO: TRIXIE! I thought you was my girl!

TRIXIE: I am! And I think you're so kind and caring to make sure none of that filthy money dirtied up your boss's impeccably manicured hands.

VITO: Yeah. That's what I was doing. Looking out for her.

(*Gwen motions for Paul puts away the Dictaphone.*)

PAUL: Looks like the machine is working just fine!

TRIXIE: Oh good! Oh. We need to get these forms to City Hall. Umm... Max? Could you bring me that box?

(*Max, gobsmacked by Trixie, comes over with a huge box of papers.*)

MAX: It is already very full.

(*Trixie takes the box.*)

TRIXIE: Oh, I have so much that needs to go over. Vito? Would you carry this for me?

(*Trixie dumps the box of papers in Vito's arms.*)

VITO: Okay.

TRIXIE: Anything else need to go?

> *(Gwen puts a box in Paul's hands.)*

GWEN: Could you mail this for me?

> *(He stacks it on Vito.)*

PAUL: I have a package I need to mail.

TRIXIE: Do you need string?

GWEN: Yes! He needs string!

TRIXIE: Sure! How much do you need? Vito, would you hold this for me?

> *(Trixie has a large spool of string on her desk. She hands Vito one end of the string.)*

VITO: Sure.

> *(Trixie points to a pair of scissors.)*

TRIXIE: Could you hand those to me?

VITO: Sure.

> *(Vito turns to grab the scissors.)*

TRIXIE: Oh, Paul! Didn't you have some plans that needed to go, too?

VITO: What?

(Vito turns around in a full circle to look at Paul and hand Trixie the scissors, wrapping the string around himself. Gwen sees what Vito has done.)

GWEN: I think he did!

MAX: Yes! He did!

(Paul runs off to fill his arms with blueprints. Gwen turns Vito to face her and places items from her purse upon the box of paperwork. Paul turns Vito to face him and dumps rolls of blueprints on top of the box. Gwen and Paul keep spinning Vito around faster and faster as everyone begins heaping more and more things onto his arms. He gets wrapped in the string. Lines

start slow then cut each other off and overlap as they spin Vito faster.)

GWEN: I have an invitation that needs to go to the comptroller's office—

PAUL: —These blueprints will need to be filed with the permits—

MAX: —Trixie, be a dear and make sure he signs all of these forms—

TRIXIE: —Yes, darling. Could you get him a pen?—

GWEN: —I know it is in here somewhere—

PAUL: —This one, too—

MAX: —Here you are Vito.—

TRIXIE: —You'll need form 536.—

VITO: —I can't hold all this.—

GWEN: —Oh, there's that compact. I thought I lost it…

PAUL: —And this should go too, just to be safe—

MAX: —In case that one doesn't work…

TRIXIE: —And form 1984—

GWEN: —Oh honestly… I know it's in here…

PAUL: —And this needs to go, too..

VITO: —How much stuff do you have?—

MAX: —Try this one.—

TRIXIE: —And form 201—

GWEN: —I just can't find that invitation—

PAUL: —And these, just to be safe—

MAX: —Well, actually, you better just hold all of these—

TRIXIE: —And 1532—

GWEN: —Hold still, I think I see it!

(Paul, Max, and Gwen spin Vito in the chair.)

VITO: I'm getting dizzy here.

TRIXIE: Oh! That's my favorite game!

MAX/PAUL/GWEN/TRIXIE: WHEEEEEE!

PAUL: That looks about right.

VITO: I can't move anything but my hands!

GWEN: How unfortunate. *(She rips the paper out of Trixie's typewriter, hands him a pen, and holds it for him to sign.)* Now, if you could just sign this.

VITO: What am I signing?

GWEN: The transcription of everything you said into the Dictaphone.

VITO: What?

TRIXIE: Wow! If I didn't know any better, it's like you wanted me to type up a confession.

VITO: What?!

(Trixie cluelessly goes into the kitchen.)

VITO: Give me that.

PAUL: Now, Vito. We have a much better plan.

VITO: Give me that!

PAUL: We have your signed confession. We have your recorded voice. BUT! We're gentlemen of reason.

VITO: Gentlemen? You blackmailing me?

PAUL: Think of this as a contractual amendment.

VITO: What do you say we settle this as gentlemen?

(Vito pulls himself out of the chair and pulls out a gun. He points it at Gwen. Vito and Paul struggle and fight. As they fight, Gwen places a call.)

PAUL: Gwen! Run!

MAX: The recording!

VITO: Ha! Ha! Ha!

(Ruby enters holding a gun.)

RUBY: Now what is going on here?

VITO: They're trying to cancel our contract, so I was just in the process of cancelling them.

> *(Trixie comes out of the kitchen humming with an armload of faded dollar bills pinned to a clothesline.)*

RUBY: What's that?

TRIXIE: Oh! The money I laundered for you and Vito. He wanted it to be a secret. Sorry, it's still a little wet.

RUBY: What?

TRIXIE: I feel bad, though, Vito. All the ink washed out.

RUBY: You gave her my money to launder?

VITO: It's not what it looks like!

MAX: You paid us with counterfeit money?

GWEN: Well, well... you know what, Paul?

PAUL: What, Gwen?

GWEN: If I'm not mistaken, I believe the deal is off!

RUBY: What?

GWEN: You gave these men sourdough! Your money isn't worth the blank paper it washed off of. They owe you nothing!

RUBY: Is that what you think? Aw. Won't the newsboys just love to hear who the police commissioner's daughter hired to build her daddy's dream project?

GWEN: You mean this "sting" operation spearheaded by one of the most brilliant minds in government?

ALL: What?

GWEN: And won't your associates just love to hear that you've been paying off all your debts with counterfeit.

RUBY: You're bluffing.

GWEN: There's a slammer full of men you've crossed with nothing but time to listen.

PAUL: And speaking of listening, we've got a little tune Vito just recorded that I think is going to be very popular.

VITO: Ignore that, Ruby...

PAUL: Would you like to hear it...?

VITO: Now... there's no reason to be hasty.

RUBY: You double-crossing… you just wait'll I tell your uncle!

> *(Police sirens wail outside the window. Vito and Ruby run over)*

RUBY: Who called the coppers?

TRIXIE: Oh! Do you think they'll want to take a look at this to see who was making bad money?

> *(Vito and Ruby turn around. Trixie drops the armload of wet money on the drafting table. The table top flips up, hitting Vito and Ruby in the chin and knocking them out the window. Trixie runs away in horror. Paul and Gwen run to the window.)*

PAUL: I guess it really is only high enough to break your legs.

MAX: You… saved us. Our little Trixie! My dear, sweet, lovely, brilliant Trixie!

VITO: *(yelling offstage)* That was a dirty trick, Trixie Fuller! I loved you!

TRIXIE: I guess this means the wedding is off…

MAX: You were going to marry that goon?

TRIXIE: He said it was the only way to keep you safe, Max…

MAX: You were going to marry him… you were going to sacrifice your own future happiness… to keep me safe…?

TRIXIE: That's what secretaries are for.

MAX: No, they're not! No they are NOT! I put my foot down, Trixie Fuller! You've pulled a lot of fast ones with me, but this is the limit! You are not marrying that man!

TRIXIE: I'm not?

MAX: Of course not! You're MY fiancé!

TRIXIE: What?

> *(Max goes over to Trixie's desk, pulls out a paperclip and bends it into a circle, gets down on one knee and asks.)*

MAX: Trixie Fuller. Would you do me the honor of being my wife?

TRIXIE: I… Yes! Yes!

> *(She flings her arms around his neck.)*

VITO: *(o.s.)* The moment I get out, Trixie, I'm coming for you! Wait for me!

MAX: That, sir, is my future wife you are talking to!
(He drops the ball peen hammer out the window.)

RUBY: *(o.s.)* OW!

MAX: Paul? I hope that you will stand up for us at the church?

TRIXIE: *(motioning to the guest chair)* But you can sit down if you like.

PAUL: Standing or sitting, you got yourself a treasure.

GWEN: We did it!

PAUL: We're behind schedule, we're broke, we'll never finish your project in time…

GWEN: And everything turned out perfect.

MAX: Absolutely perfect.

> *(Gwen kisses Paul and Max kisses Trixie simultaneously.)*

MAX: This calls for a celebration! *(Max picks up a stack of paper and throws it into the sky.)*   Coffee's on me!

> *(Paul turns on the radio. They laugh and dance and throw more paper and use staplers as castanets. Trixie picks up a stack of papers to throw. She stops.)*

TRIXIE: Oh! I forgot to give you these.

MAX: What are they?

PAUL: A stack of job acceptances!

TRIXIE: I found some of your old designs and just submitted them. I used to do that a lot for your father.

MAX: We've got work for the next ten years!

TRIXIE: Funny how that worked out.

MAX, GWEN, & PAUL: TRIXIE!!

> *(Max swings Trixie around and Gwen and Paul throw the papers joyously in the air.)*

(END OF PLAY)

VOCABULARY

Bread - Money

Butter & Eggs Man - The man with the bankroll. Also a rural dweller who comes in to the city and throws money around in a showy fashion to seem rich and important.

Dempsey Dumpsters - Dumpsters used to be called "Dempseys" for the brand, like tissue is called "Kleenex."

Eggs in Coffee - Run smoothly

Mitt Me Kid! - Congratulate me (usually accompanied with a handshake)

Nuts! - Telling someone they are full of nonsense

Slammer - Jail

Sourdough - Counterfeit money

5 for 4 - 20% interest (You'll give them $5 for the loan of $4.) Historically this was what the mob charged their borrowers.

About the Playwright

Kate Danley is an award winning novelist and USA TODAY bestselling author. She has been honored with the Garcia Award for Best Fiction Book of the Year (*The Woodcutter*), McDougall Previews Award for Best Fantasy Book of the Year (*Queen Mab*), and her series *Maggie MacKay: Magical Tracker* has been optioned for film and television development. She has sold over half-a-million books globally and her plays have been produced in New York, Los Angeles, Bath (UK), Chicago, Seattle, Houston, and Baltimore. Her play *Building Madness* won the 2016 Panowski Playwriting Award. She graduated from Towson University and trained at RADA London, The Groundlings, Folger Shakespeare, Theatricum Botanicum, Acme, and Seattle Rep. She performed her original stand-up at such clubs as The Comedy Store and The Icehouse and wrote sketch for a weekly show in Hollywood. She won the Breckenridge Festival of Film Screenplay Competition for her feature script *Fairy Blood*. Her shorts *The Playhouse, Dog Days, Sock Zombie, SuperPout,* and *Sports Scents* can be seen in festivals and on the internet.